Unbounded Organizing in Community

Unbounded Organizing in Community

Gavin Andersson, Howard Richards

2015

Dignity Press
World Dignity University Press

*Dedicated to our colleagues at the
Seriti Institute*

© 2015 Gavin Andersson, Howard Richards

This work is published under the Creative Commons Attribution-NonCommercial-ShareAlike 4.0 International (CC BY-NC-SA 4.0) license. Details can be found at: http://creativecommons.org/licenses/by-nc-sa/4.0/

Published by Dignity Press
http://www.dignitypress.org
16 Northview Ct.
Lake Oswego, OR 97035
USA

To contact the authors or to order, go to the book's web page: www.dignitypress.org/unbounded

ISBN 978-1-937570-60-6 (print)
ebook versions:
ISBN 978-1-937570-61-3 (ePub)
ISBN 978-1-937570-62-0 (Kindle)

Contents

Chapter One:
What We Ask of Our Readers,
and What We Offer Them   **9**

   Where We Are   10
   Organizing   10
      Organization is Power   10
   Community   12
   The Readers This Book Is for   13
   What We Offer   14
   Our Sources   15

Chapter Two:
Introducing the Organization Workshop   **17**

   The Experience   17
   The Question   19
   Practical Learning Exercise   19
   The Answer   20
   Practical Learning Exercise   25

Chapter Three:
Clodomir Santos de Morais   **25**

   Brazil in the 1960s   26
   The Month-Long Clandestine Meeting in Recife   26
   Learning from Practice: The Follow-up Study   28
   Practical Learning Exercise   30

Chapter Four:
The Beginning of an
Organization Workshop — 31

   Step One: The Invitation — 31
   Step Two: Scoping — 33
   Practical Learning Exercise — 35
     But Why So Many Participants? — 36
   Step Three: Getting It Together — 36
   Step Four: The Director's Opening Speech — 37
     What Does the Director Say in the Opening Speech? — 38
   Practical Learning Exercise — 40

Chapter Five:
Learning Organizing by Organizing — 45

   The Crew Talks Business Only With the PE — 46
   Some Problems Maybe Nobody Thought of — 48
   The First Lectures — 51
   Excerpts from the First Lectures — 51
   Practical Learning Exercise — 53

Chapter Six:
Unbounded Organization — 55

   First Practical Exercise: Questioning the Box — 62
   Second Practical Exercise: A Practical Step Forward,
     Organizing a Personal Network — 62
   Third Practical Exercise : What pattern of activities
     can we create together? — 64

Chapter Seven:
Unbounded Community Development   **65**

  Four Practical Exercises   68
    First Exercise: Study What Is in the People's Heads   68
    Second Exercise: Take Notes on Energies.
      In Other Words, Take Notes on Emotions and
      Feelings   69
    Third Practical Exercise: Brainstorm Possible
      Projects by Connecting Gifts   70
    Fourth Practical Exercise: A Homework Assignment   72

Chapter Eight:
Alignment   **73**

  Organizing *For* Rather Than Organizing *Against*   76
  Practical Exercises   78
    First Practical Exercise: Planting Trees   78
    Second Practical Exercise: Keep Bees,
      or Run an Organic Garden   79
    Third Practical Exercise: A Topic for Discussion   80
    Fourth Practical Exercise: Two Questions   80

Chapter Nine:
Meetings   **81**

  Meetings for Business   81
    Beginning the Meeting   82
    Running the Meeting   83
    Ending the Meeting   84
  Meetings for Learning   85

Tense Meetings	86
Practical Learning Exercises	88
First Practical Exercise: A Day-Long Meeting to Map a Community's Assets	88
Second Practical Exercise: A Topic for Discussion	90

Chapter Ten:
Bokfontein Amazes the Nations — 91

Alignment in Action	91
The Next Steps Are Unbounded	95
Practical Learning Exercise: A Community Time Line	96

Appendix:
Suggestions for Further Reading — 99

Chapter One: What We Ask of Our Readers, and What We Offer Them

> What we ask of our readers is
> *imagination, realism,* and *good will.*

Imagination to envision that the way things are is not the way things have to be.

Realism to see the world as it is:
Even when reality is different from what the mainstream media and the dominant culture say it is, and even when reality is different from what we ourselves wish were true.

Good will to want to make a difference for good in the world.

> The past cannot be changed.
>
> Reality is now.
>
> The future is ours to construct.
>
> No amount of complaining
> will give us a better past.
>
> No amount of dreaming, without action,
> will give us a better future.

Where We Are

We all live in our own little corners of the world. Here, Now, This room. These people. Yet it is one world. One planet we all live on. One air we all breathe.

One human family, all descendants of one woman who lived on the eastern side of Africa some 140,000 to 200,000 years ago.

What we do in our little corners of the world can make a difference for the whole world.

This is one message of this book.

Organizing

Organization is Power

For our present purposes we can define "organization" as "getting together to do things we cannot do alone". we believe that it is the ability to *organize on our own behalf* that enables groups of people to live with purpose, self-belief and dignity. Organization is the key social skill of human beings, but can be lost or forgotten in modern society.

We always start organizing something particular, here in our little corner of the world where we are. For example, the authors of this book – one or both of them – have organized:

- A high school humour magazine
- A band

- A church group
- A regional magazine
- A philosophical discussion club
- A business (more than one)
- A cooperative owned and run by its members (again more than one)
- A labour union (again more than one)
- A political campaign for public office
- Underground resistance against *apartheid*
- A secondary school curriculum
- A network of grassroots study circles
- A university Peace and Global Studies degree programme
- A university degree programme in Business and Non-profit Management
- A neighbourhood association
- A non-profit foundation (again more than one)
- Adult education in parent-effectiveness

Readers may find it hard to believe that the writers have had so much organizing experience. But remember that there are two of us, and we've learnt how to work with others. Then of course we are both pretty old. Both of us have had time over the years to do a number of different things.

We believe that the *basic skills to organize effectively* can be learned.

The purpose of this book is to help the reader to learn them.

Community

Acquiring organizing skills positions us to improve the quality of life in our *community*, including improving levels of trust and mutual support between people.

'*Community*' is a word that can be used without thinking. Very often we mean a *community of place*; where everyone living in a specific area is seen as part of 'the community.' But of course there may be great divisions between people living in a common area so that it is difficult to think of them as one community: there are those with more power and influence, those who are richer, those who came to live there only recently, and there may be differences of race, religion, politics or background. We can talk of a '*community of interest*' to cover all those affected by an issue. Or we may have a '*community of practice*', where we refer to people working or learning on a common theme or issue. If we consider the phrase 'community development' in the light of these three meanings, we suggest that organization can easily move beyond physical boundaries, and that the key to development (of people or of places) is a conscious effort to forge a community of interest and of practice.

Communication is central to any effort to work together, and as people start talking to each other a spirit of community flourishes.

Take for example a community development programme where Howard worked in Chile. When it began, people would refer to a neighbour as "the one in the red shirt" because they did not know his name. As the community developed, people got to know each other. They helped each other out. They worked together. They had a vision. They had projects. There was more of what in African tradition is called *ubuntu*. "I am because you are".

Bishop Desmond Tutu wrote that it is not really possible to translate the full meaning of *ubuntu* into a modern European language like English. We suggest that sometimes a good translation is "community".

As we work successfully to organize communities, people become more secure, safer, and happier.

The Readers This Book Is For

It may already be obvious that we write for those who are interested in organizing beyond their immediate households. We assume our readers want to organize communities for the common good; to help communities organize on their own behalf. We write especially for those who are inspired by love of their neighbour, love of Nature and who have a healthy self-love.

We will be drawing ideas from our experience in the little corners of the world where we have been and where we are now, and from our studies, for the benefit of readers who can try these ideas out – and modify them to fit their own local realities – in the little corners of the world where they are.

Learning how to organize, like learning a sport, learning to play a musical instrument, or learning anything else, takes practice. We will be suggesting practical learning exercises for the reader.

We know that many people do not read books, and rather learn by being drawn into discussion and organization by others.

We are therefore looking for readers who care about this 'non-reading' majority and who are able to communicate with them. This is a book about organizing in your corner of the world in ways that fit in with the good of the whole world. We will argue that even these 'little' efforts need to draw in as many people as possible, and we will share stories about a method which aims to draw in hundreds of people in changing the way things are done where they live.

The readers we are writing for are motivated. This is a book for people who want to do something in life, and who are ready to work to do it.

What We Offer

We know that apathy is a fact. There is apathy all around us. There is lack of communication, and there is disorder, discouragement, loneliness. In one word there is "disorganization". In three words there is "lack of community". We (the authors) have been living in a world full of apathy all our lives and we have something to say about how to triumph over apathy in ourselves and in others.

Part of learning to organize is learning how to liberate the genius of people, who have been frustrated by material poverty, the suffocation of their own value systems and ideas, and a lack of accountability from those who shape their lives. This frustration can lead to frozen motivation and a lack of self-belief. Frozen motivation can be liberated, by the simple act of performing a piece of work with someone else.

Or true love.

Or by an exciting conversation.

These are just three examples, but if you think about your own life you will easily find some more ...

There are numerous university degree programmes, books, and scientific journals about organization. We flatter ourselves – call this healthy self-love – that we have something new to say.

We call it Unbounded Organization. We will talk more about this later, but in essence we mean organization across society, not just the activities we do within a club, or association, or church group. (And we also mean that our own organization can involve others in its activities.)

We offer the reader not just an introduction to the science of organization, but also *a cutting edge introduction to new thinking.*

Our Sources

We will be drawing on many experiences and studies, but especially on experience from the Organization Workshop.

Gavin has directed more than twenty Organization Workshops in Botswana and South Africa. An Organization Workshop is a four to six week-long work experience where participants learn to organize by organizing, and which creates enterprises and new ways of living in a community.

In addition to doing practical work, participants in an Organization Workshop go through daily study sessions that draw on the *Notes towards a Theory of Organization* that were originally written by the Brazilian educator, lawyer, and activist

Clodomir Santos de Morais in the early 1960s, and which have been added to by two people since then. We will share a little about de Morais and the OW, because the ideas that were first shared by de Morais are the starting point for our Unbounded theory. We reckon this is useful to understand the organizing you and I are doing now, here where we are, *in the context of the whole evolution of the human species on planet earth.*

Chapter Two: Introducing the Organization Workshop

The Experience

Let's learn more about Organization Workshops.

Imagine you are at one.

Close your eyes to prepare to see something in imagination.

(Don't keep them closed too long or you will not be able to read the next words on this page!)

An Organization Workshop (OW for short) lasts about a month or even 6 weeks.

Imagine it is the second to last day of an OW. You are there.

Now please close your eyes again.

Imagine you are in Botswana.

You are on the outskirts of Otse. You could call Otse a large village or a small town. About three thousand people live there.

It is early in the morning, just after sunrise.

Now open your eyes. What do you see?

You see an organized community in action!

There it is! An Organization Workshop. It is being held in and around a cluster of small buildings on a hillside on the outskirts of the village.

Some people are finishing breakfast. Others are standing in line to take a shower. A delivery truck arrives. It has come back from town after making a first delivery of fresh-baked bread. The aroma from the second batch of bread fills the air.

You see a storeroom where tools are kept. Members of each work team are checking out the equipment they will need for the day.

The welding team, made up mostly of women who have learnt welding over the last three weeks, lays out the steel for the burglar-proofing it plans to make for the storeroom.

A work team of builders starts to plaster the walls of an extension to the building where the bakery operates.

Another team prepares to put gutters on the roof of the newly built food processing room.

You see carpenters continuing where they left off the previous day, installing shelves in the storeroom. Another work team starts putting up the fence around the site where a bandages factory is to be built.

The driver – just back from delivering bread – moves the truck for his next task. Five people load the truck with trees they will plant today a few kilometres away at the kgotla (the village meeting place.)

Looking farther up the hillside, you see the agriculture team working on terraces and contour banks. The idea is to harvest rainwater and channel it so it doesn't wash away the hillside. (Botswana is a dry country where every drop of water is precious.)

Everywhere you look you see purposeful activity! Everybody – more than a hundred people in all – knows what to do and why they are doing it. Everyone knows what is required of her/ him for the day, yet there is nobody who seems to be giving instructions.

The Question

How did this happen???

A month ago the people you just watched swinging into action at the start of their work day were for the most part disorganized and unmotivated like so many others we have seen in so many places around the globe.

There were heavy doses of discouragement and apathy.

    Not to mention _____!

> ### Practical Learning Exercise.
> *What are we not mentioning? Fill in the blank space from your own experience. What do disorganized, unmotivated, discouraged, apathetic people do?*

Now, a month later, *over a hundred people – in some OWs over a thousand – are part of a single coordinated enterprise.*

They have organized a bakery. They have put up new buildings. They have improved their community. They are well on their way to creating terraces on the hillside. They have plans for a bandages factory.

To repeat the question:

How did this happen?

How can we understand the process from the first day of the OW to this point just near its end that has produced such a change?

The participants arrived with no experience of complex organization, and the majority of them have low levels of literacy, and few practical skills. Now they are a productive and self-organized enterprise

Did this happen by chance? Was it just good luck?
Or was it a miracle?

The Answer

What happened over the weeks did not happen just by chance. It was not just good luck. It was not a miracle. There is a theory behind every step in an OW. It is no accident that not just at Otse, Botswana, but for half a century in hundreds of OWs in hundreds of places on three continents people have learned to organize by organizing.

Not every OW organizes a bakery. Not every OW harvests rainwater. Not every OW teaches women how to weld. There is different practical work in each of them. But in every OW people *learn organization*. They learn how to organize themselves together to do things they cannot do alone. They share a narrative about organization since the beginning of time, and they draw on a common theory of organization.

We have generalized the theory behind the Organization Workshop to a theory of *Unbounded Organization* (UO for short).

There is nothing so practical as a good theory.

What you do in your little corner of the world may and may not be an OW. But we are confident that whatever you are doing, if you learn and apply the principles of Unbounded Organization you will be a better organizer. We believe – and this is why we are writing this book – that what we have learned from our experience you can apply to your experience. Hopefully you will improve the method as you practice it – and pass it on to someone else improved!

It may seem that we are making a rash promise, one that we cannot keep. But as you learn more you will see that our promise is perfectly reasonable – it is entirely reasonable for you to organize in an unbounded way. As we have said earlier, you will need to use your creative imagination, be realistic, and be motivated by good intentions.

The principles of Unbounded Organization are not hard to understand. They are common sense enriched by experience and study.

The method of the Organization Workshop was pioneered by Clodomir de Morais. He taught it to Ivan Labra. Ivan Labra taught it to Gavin Andersson.

Doing Organization Workshops was one of the experiences that led Gavin to the idea of Unbounded Organization.

The next chapter tells about Clodomir de Morais.

Practical Learning Exercise

Bad habits are heatedly discussed in organization workshops. Everybody has something to say about them. Clodomir de Morais profiled some typical bad habits:

Consider the individualist opportunist. The individualist opportunist believes only in the individual. He always puts himself above the organization. She does not believe in organized action. She or he acts alone and wants it that way. In meetings the individualist opportunist does not listen to anybody. He or she claims the power to monopolise the right to speak for the time she or he pleases. The individualist is looking for how to put his or her interests before the interests of the rest.

Consider the bad habits of someone who has no sense of time, who can be called a "spontaneist". The spontaneist is obstinate in his opposition to planning. She wants to do the things that are pleasant when it pleases her. The spontaneist does not plan anything, He lives for now, on the basis of his personal interest. Whenever a member proposes planning a specific action, the spontaneist gets annoyed, even angry. For her the watch is a piece of jewellery. He does not have a specific time or hour for anything. If a member asks "When are we going to do this?" she replies: "anytime!", or "one of these days". His dates are vague, undefined. The spontaneist is terrified of planned action and cannot take it when planning establishes fixed dates for controlling the work.

Consider the destroyer. The destroyer is opposed to the organization of people's actions. He does not account for tools or other resources he uses. She is a disorganized person. He manages a large enterprise as if it were a corner shop. The money comes in and the money goes out but she does not record anything. A meeting led by somebody with a destroyer tendency is chaotic. When this tendency dominates, the members act like a crowd at a soccer match pushing to buy drinks.

Do any of these profiles remind you of someone you know?

What other bad habits make life miserable for the co-workers in an organization?

Are there common habits that you can identify amongst people with whom you work or live?

Chapter Three: Clodomir Santos de Morais

Clodomir Santos de Morais is a black Brazilian. He was born in 1928. He is still alive, getting close to 90.

He was born in the poverty-stricken rural North East of Brazil. His father sent him to a local trade school to learn to be a tailor. Driven by poverty and drawn by the excitement of the big city, he ran away to Sao Paulo.

In Sao Paulo he did whatever he could find. He learned saxophone and played jazz in clubs. He became a part time reporter for a newspaper. Then he got a steady job as an assembly line worker on the conveyor belt at Ford Motor Company. He worked his way up to line supervisor. He was a union man. He joined an underground political party: The Communists.

Meanwhile he continued his education to a matric level. He studied in a Catholic Salesian school, then in a Protestant Adventist school. He was expelled three times but he kept coming back.

With his big city experience under his belt he returned to his family and to his roots in the rural North East. Building on his newspaper experience he created his own news agency. He made enough money to send himself to law school. He entered politics. He was elected to be an MP in the provincial parliament.

Brazil in the 1960s

The time we are talking about is the 1960s. *Apartheid in South Africa. War in Vietnam. Flower power in California. The Beatles in the UK. Class struggle in Brazil.*

During the first years of the 1960s Brazil was supposed to be a democracy. It was supposed to be a democracy but the real power was in the hands of a few ruling families. *You have to understand this if you are going to understand how the Organization Workshops began.*

You have to understand that even though Clodomir de Morais was a lawyer and an MP he had to make sure to keep one step ahead of the hired thugs and the secret police. He could easily "disappear". Many activists have "disappeared" at different times and places.

You have to understand that even though the farm workers and the smallholders who worked their own land were supposed to have legal rights, *if they wanted to try to get respect for their rights they had to organize secretly.*

This is where the ideas behind the Organization Workshop began. *They came from a month-long secret meeting to teach how to use the law to uphold the rights of farm workers.*

The Month-Long Clandestine Meeting in Recife

The meeting was held in a private home in the city of Recife. You can find Recife on a map of Brazil in the North East corner of the country, not too far from the mouth of the Amazon River. At the time of the meeting the areas of town where poor people lived were patrolled by police, who were there to prevent any political activity.

The purpose of the meeting was for activists to spend a month learning the laws concerning agrarian reform. If the activists knew the legal rights of those struggling for land, then this could guide organizing strategy and help secure their right to land.

The 45 participants arrived for the secret course in agrarian law one at a time over a period of several days. *They did not arrive all at once because they did not want to alert the police and their spies about the underground law course.*

When at last they were all gathered together they had to *organize* daily life. *Forty-five people had to live quietly in one house for a month – because if they made any noise this would show that something was happening in the house.* They had to organize sleeping space and laundry. They had to organize times for each person to wash and for going to the toilet. They had to schedule cooking the food in the pantry so it would not all be eaten in the first days leaving nothing for the last days. People took turns to prepare food, wash dishes, and clean house. Material for each part of the course had to be reproduced and shared, then studied in groups and in joint discussions. Tasks had to be distributed, work planned, and performance monitored. Recreation had to be organized: Games and story-telling, since relaxation is as necessary as work. Departures had to be organized so that the participants could leave as they had come, one by one over a period of several days.

Clodomir de Morais reflected on this experience when he went round to visit the participants in their home villages. He found that some people had forgotten some parts of what they had learnt about agrarian law, while some shared that they had learned little or nothing that they did not know already. However *every participant had learned about organization*. The rhythms of activity in the learning event had provided them with all the skills and tools to become an organizer and in some cases they were achieving wonders by facilitating organization in their home situation.

Learning from Practice: The Follow-up Study

Clodomir Santos de Morais reflected on this unexpected effect. He began to think that one key to the learning about organization had been the need to share a common pool of resources and to practice *a division of labour* amongst the participants as they worked out how to do the hundreds of small tasks necessary to stay together in peaceful learning community for a month. He began to consider how to use the insights he had gained to create a method where more people could learn about organization. Over the next years he designed and ran scores of experimental workshops in the Peasant Leagues of Brazil. Here the participants shared a common pool of resources, like land and tools. As they worked they learnt how to analyze each job and allocate tasks, becoming more efficient in their use of labour and time. De Morais started to develop a theory of organization which he shared in the workshops, based on his own life experiences and his reading.

He had learned at Ford Motor Company that there is a *big difference* between the *mental attitude* of a worker who is part of a team where each contributes a small part to making the final product and the mental attitude of the artisan who makes something working alone from start to finish. (He had experienced the artisan's mental attitude when he first learned how to be a tailor).

He put his reflections on these experiences together with what he had learned from reading.

One part of his reading was the Marxist classics. They made him aware that the way things are done here and now is not the way things have always been done everywhere. In different places at different times *people have organized themselves to work together to meet their needs in many different ways.*

Later de Morais studied psychology, particularly the work of Leont'ev, a Russian cognitive psychologist. Leont'ev worked within a tradition started by Lev Vygotsky, which is now referred to as Activity Theory. This school of psychology observed that physical activity is suggested by the tools available – so that a group of children will paint pictures if given paint and brushes and paper. De Morais found here another scientific explanation for the participants learning organization i.e. that *a common pool of resources stimulates shared activity*. Principles he was deriving from reflection on his own experiences were thus confirmed and enhanced by his reading.

De Morais' practical experiences and theoretical reflections came together in the idea of an *Organization Workshop*. In the next chapter we will outline how one begins.

Practical Learning Exercise

Keep a notebook to help you to reflect on your own experiences. Besides learning from experience over the years and months try to learn from experience every day. Pay particular attention to how you work together with other people. Here is an example:

What did I do well today, and why? I told a joke everybody laughed at and liked. It was the right thing to say at the right time to clear the air and help us move forward as a team.

What did I do wrong today, and why? I forgot it was my friend's birthday, because I do not keep a record of birthdays.

How then can I improve? In my notebook I can store witticisms to use on appropriate occasions. I can mark my friends' birthdays on a calendar that hangs where I will see it every day. I can write down the criticism and then reflect on it later when I am not angry, and see what I can learn about myself.

*Note: We often reflect on what went badly, but when things go well we might not remember to reflect on that. And although we may say something went well, or badly, we usually do not go deeper to ask why exactly this was so. To learn how to improve our behaviour (or performance in a work setting) it is always useful to look at what went well and what went badly **as well as the reasons for this**.*

Chapter Four: The Beginning of an Organization Workshop

Clodomir de Morais invented the Organization Workshop in Brazil in the 1960s. After that he directed OWs in Central America, in Portugal and in other places. We will explain how OWs are done today in southern Africa, because this is a way to talk about some of the core skills for organizing in community. We don't expect the reader to try to organize an OW, but we do hope that reading about it will show how much people can achieve by working together. We will describe how one begins in terms of FOUR STEPS.

Step One: The Invitation

First comes an invitation from organized parts of a community, and an agreement to run an OW.

Why is an invitation needed? Because an OW works best when leading actors in a community

1. Know it has problems to tackle (or major opportunities to respond to.)
2. Are willing to work to resolve its problems.
3. Are united enough to agree on the invitation.
4. Are interested to try new methods of community organizing.

COMMENTS:

1. There are methods for raising collective awareness of the problems of a community as well as the strengths (assets) that are available. We prefer the methods that focus on the positive by "mapping" the resources the community has and potential solutions to its problems. Our preferred approach is called "asset-based". Later in this book we give some exercises that show how to do community mapping.

2. There needs to be clear commitment from INSIDE the community itself. The common feature in all failed organization is a lack of interest or commitment from those who are assumed to benefit from it. *If the community is divided, where one group wants the OW and another group does not – it is better to* BACK OFF.

3. People need some idea of what is proposed with an OW: This may come out of a detailed description of the process in meetings or because of something someone has heard.

4. Somebody in the community might have become enthusiastic about OW because of hearing about it from a cousin in some place where an OW has already been held. In every place the OW has brought good results, doing things like providing water, through people re organizing to prevent violence, to creating enterprises[*]. The fact that a community is united enough to think about an OW does not mean there can't be more advances in organization. In fact the OW will bring

---

[*] The website www.seriti.org.za lists achievements of OWs in South Africa over a period of five to six years.

stronger organization and improve life in the community. It will also enable new leaders to emerge; and it is useful to prepare existing leaders to welcome this fact rather than instinctively opposing any new leadership.

Step Two: Scoping

The Scoping of the OW is the set of tasks that enables the design of the process and specifically answers the following questions: How many people should attend? What work there is for them to do? What technical training or support will they need? How much money is needed for all this to happen, and where will this come from?

One part of scoping the OW is to meet with as many different organizations and individuals in the community as possible. Even if you live in the community that you are scoping it is necessary to see issues from other people's eyes and hear about things from different perspectives. To do scoping, the team members spend time in the community; walk around, talk to people, meet with all kinds of community groups and organizations, visit the clinic, the school, churches. Talk to the small trader selling sweets and fruit; sit in on the unemployed men's discussions at the bar, attend choir practice with the teenage girls. The object is to find out what people think works well and should be increased, what needs to be done, and what *could be* done: Both the priority tasks to tackle a problem, and the exciting dreams for change in the community.

Sometimes an outsider can see potential where someone living in the community does not do so and so it is always useful to bring some people with particular skills into the scoping team.

A steep hillside might look to an agriculturalist as potential terraced land supporting crops, whereas for those in the community it was simply a rocky place. A broken earth dam may provoke an engineer to look for a better site a little way away, and to think about simple ways of constructing a sturdy wall. And then of course, the local government will have made plans, and some parts of them will not have been tackled for various reasons. Ideas for change can then start from different starting points and conversations. Whatever ideas emerge it is always necessary to share them with people, in community forums, to get their reactions.

Once you have a sense of the different work that can be done it is possible to choose the specific jobs that will be undertaken in the OW. Ideally you should break up big pieces of work into manageable 'blocks'/jobs that can be done by a work team in a period of a few weeks. There should be enough different kinds of work that people will have to divide labour and resources (tools, time, transport etc) to see that each job gets done. This is the first requirement for learning organization; in short, the mixture of jobs to be completed must require co-ordination of the efforts of different people.

The next phase in the scoping is to create a technical plan for each job. One job might be, for example, repairing the roof of a frail care home. You will need to break down the job into its different tasks, see what tools and materials are needed for the task, how many people are needed to do it and how long they will take. You will also need to see what if any technical backup is needed (e.g. a Carpenter showing how to repair the roof trusses). If you do not know much about the work to be done and cannot therefore do this work analysis, then you will need the help of someone who does know. In southern Africa most OWs have a small technical crew made up of people who are experienced in this.

The scoping has to be detailed enough to be used to make *work offers*, stating what work is to be done. The agreement about what the pay will be comes from a negotiation between the facilitators (the crew) and the participants enterprise once the OW has started, and gets summarised in a contract.

> ### Practical Learning Exercise
>
> Look at different pieces of work that need to be done in the community where you live. Plan the steps of a piece of work that will take five people one month to complete.

If there are going to be 200 participants in the OW, then it is necessary to scope enough work to keep all of them busy for the time of the OW. Put differently, to decide how many people can participate we need to know the amount of work available, and the budget for tools, material and payment of labour. Sometimes there may be 500 or even a thousand people at an OW.

But Why So Many Participants?

First of all, there is much more pressure to *learn organization* when there are large numbers of people involved, whereas it is pretty easy to organize 20 or 30 people to work. Second we want participants to learn about complex organization, and they can only do this within a complex organization. Third, we want people who have been isolated and more or less on-their-own to learn the *mental attitudes* that go with being effective and successful in the real world today – and today we live in a society of organizations and so need to learn about the behaviours that will help or harm those organizations.

Does this mean that if I am organizing on a small scale, with a few people only, then this book is irrelevant for me?

It was Gavin's specific experience directing *Organization Workshops* that sparked thinking about the ideas of *Unbounded Organization*. That is why we are writing first about OW to start communicating the general ideas of UO. When you learn (*and practice!*) the general principles of UO you can apply them in any kind of organization on any scale – from the smallest to the largest.

Step Three: Getting It Together

The participants in the workshop have to be identified, registered and assembled. This can be relatively easy if the community issuing the invitation already had in mind who would participate, but it is always important to make sure that all groups have a chance to comment or nominate, so the participants represent different communities of interest.

A right mix of participants will include those with different work backgrounds, as well as those with little work experience. It will bring together young and old, women and men, in the same proportions as exist more broadly in the community.

On the day that the OW begins, all the equipment, tools, materials, vehicles, technical resources and money to pay labour should be on site. In addition accommodation should be ready, as well as an office for the participants' enterprise and another one for the crew, a secure storeroom, and a hall/tent big enough for all the participants to meet together – as well as a public address system.

Step Four: The Director's Opening Speech

On the first day of the OW when the people are gathered together for the opening, the director – the coordinator of the OW crew – makes an opening speech.

> The first director back in Brazil in the early 1960s was Clodomir de Morais. Then Brazil fell under a brutal military dictatorship and de Morais spent some time in jail. Upon release he sneaked into the embassy of Chile and escaped. He was soon hired by the United Nations to run Organization Workshops in Central America and then in other countries. In Central America Ian Cherrett from Holland, Ivan Labra from Chile, and others who worked under de Morais learned how to be a director. Ian was the first to direct an OW in Africa. Ivan ran many OWs in Africa and trained Gavin Andersson who in turn trained Terry Grove, Aaron Maselwane and Sibusiso Mkhize in the Seriti Institute OW programme. Seriti Institute has put the director at the head of a crew, sometimes also called the Facilitators' Enterprise. We are hoping that this book will help the formation of OW directors and crew by putting some of the main ideas in writing – but there is no substitute for experience.

What Does the Director Say in the Opening Speech?

Something like this:

- This is not the same kind of course that you have attended before. It is a course for adults who can assume responsibility for their actions. *It is a workshop in the true sense: You will work and be able to earn money for your work. The main focus of the workshop is for you to learn about organization, and this means practical work.*

- When we leave you, in a few minutes from now, you must organize yourselves into an enterprise. You can organize any way you like; it is up to you. Draw up your rules for taking decisions and for managing money, so these are clear from the start. You will probably have to show these rules to the bank manager if you want to open a bank account.

- When you are organized we will loan to you all the tools, machinery, vehicles and offices. We will require the representatives of the newly created enterprise to sign for each item by means of a detailed inventory, and if anything is missing or broken when you give these back to us at the end of the OW you will have to pay for it. Your enterprise will also have access to certain support services: Typist, driver, childcare specialist et cetera.

- We have put up a description of each of the many jobs that are available for you to work on. Don't do any work unless you have a contract with us. We will pay at market rates for each job, so if you organize very well you will be able to carry some money home at the end.

- Participants are expected to work a minimum of six hours a day, but you can work longer if you wish.

- The consumption of alcohol or any kind of intoxication is prohibited.
- The crew (the Facilitators' Enterprise) has organized food for the first three days to allow the participants to form their organization. After the third day the cooks will leave and we will hand over the kitchen to you. You will have to choose some amongst you to cook, and some of the money you earn will have to be spent on food.
- The crew (FE) will deliver lectures on the *Theory of Organization* every day for one and a half hours for the first 16 days (a total of some 24 hours). This is compulsory for all participants and a register of attendance will be kept. The FE will respond to requests for further training courses, which the participants enterprise deems necessary and asks for in writing.
- Everything that occurs during the workshop needs to be recorded and compiled by the participants in a final document or Memory Book. This must be reproduced so that each one of the participants can take home a copy at the end of the workshop. (*Included in this book will be a full copy of the Notes to a Theory of Organization* by Clodomir de Morais *which will be the content for our learning sessions during the next sixteen days.*)
- The crew is responsible for management of a crèche for your children. We have early childhood development specialists to run this crèche but they will need help from child carers. Those of you who want to learn about running a crèche may choose to take up these positions.
- The speech ends with the director reminding participants that they are there on a voluntary basis. "If anybody does not like these conditions of the workshop, s/he can leave

now. If you don't leave now then you can only leave the site once your new enterprise has established rules."

In the next chapter we will learn more about how an OW works and the principles behind how it works.

> ### Practical Learning Exercise
>
> One part of the exercise of mapping a community's assets and problems is to go door to door to talk to people. Why not practise doing this?
>
> You may be part of an organization and want to see what people would like the organization to do, or you may simply want to understand what ideas people have to improve life in the community.
>
> HERE IS SOME ADVICE (drawn from our experience):
>
> 1. Go in pairs.
> 2. *At least one of you should be well known there so people will not feel they are talking to strangers.* Alternatively you may need to wear the badge or uniform of a local organization.

3. You will need a "story". A "story" is a short explanation of who you are, why you are there, and who (if anybody) is paying you. Almost everyone will want to know what you are going to do with the information you get, and you had better think carefully about this. Do not promise to change things yourself, but do work out how you will try to use the information for the good of the community.
4. *Listen. Draw people out with questions and comments.*
5. Start with small talk. Get into the heavy issues later.
6. *Do not take notes while people are talking. If it is OK with them, you can record. Some people like to be recorded.*
7. Follow up their leads. Encourage them to say more about what concerns them.
8. Do not be discouraged if somebody slams a door in your face, gets mad, or just refuses to see you. *This is normal. Keep polite no matter how rude someone is to you.*
9. Repeat what someone just told you and ask them to say more about it.
10. Although the main point is listening, it helps to have some success stories in the back of your mind to fit into the conversation where appropriate. *Many people know their community has problems, but they need to be convinced that it is worth the effort to ORGANIZE to do something about them.*

Here are some examples of success stories:
- In Riemvasmaak: People got together to use an unused structure for childminding and a crèche, freeing up women to work.
- In Munsieville people were able to get access to a seven-hectare piece of land for an agricultural project. (Getting access to land for community projects is easier than you might think – as is shown by experience in many places.)
- In Ntambanana they started a poultry rearing project. One of the spin-offs is manure for gardens.
- From Alexandra, part of Johannesburg: Community organizations started a "Today he brought her flowers" campaign to mobilise society against the scourge of violence against women. This campaign touched a nerve and support spread to the broader community, with a number of taxi drivers joining the campaign. More women came forward to report abuse.

11. Cheer people up. Do not leave anybody more depressed than they already were.
12. Show that you care and that you are listening to what they are saying.
13. If you are going to do a survey with a questionnaire, do informal conversations first. The informal conversations will help you to phrase the questions for the survey. Make sure the questionnaire is not too long!

14. Whether or not you record what people say, you should write up notes as soon as you get back to home or office before you forget the details of what people said and how they felt.
15. Date your notes.
16. If your notes are on paper (instead of on a computer) leave blank space so you can come back to them later to add new insights on the same topics.
17. Try to get contact information about people but do not push them if they are reluctant. Once you get a list of contacts, review it every month or so to make sure you are staying in touch with these people and not losing the relationship by failing to keep it active.
18. Take your time. It takes time for people to get used to you, to the way you look, to the sound of your voice, to the words you use (your vocabulary.)
19. Actually you should be using their vocabulary more and your own vocabulary less, as you gradually learn their vocabulary.
20. What you learn from one person try out on other people. Check what people think of each other's ideas.

This is enough for now. We hope it was helpful. We are aware that these pointers drawn from our experience may and may not be relevant to your situation.

Chapter Five:
Learning Organizing by Organizing

Imagine that you are at an OW on its third day.

You are in a hall that the community has provided for the OW meeting place. This may be a school hall at a time when school is on vacation. Often this is a community centre.

Just after lunch today you were present when tools and vehicles were handed over to your Participants' Enterprise (PE).

Your PE got a fully equipped office, a storeroom and some working capital.

There is so much cash that one thing is obvious. The PE will have to open a bank account immediately.

The feeling of excitement is still in the air. There are a LOT of tools.

They make you aware that a LOT of work can be done.

Work offers are taped on a wall. Each one requires a team of people. Participants are looking at them and telling their elected leaders which jobs they would like to do. The leaders, grouped in a "Committee", get ready to negotiate contracts with the crew. Each contract will specify what exactly is to be done in each job and what the pay will be when it is done.

To be paid the Participants' Enterprise (PE) has to sign a contract with the crew (the OW Facilitators). Then the work has to be done, inspected and approved, before the invoice from the PE will be paid.

Walking around a bit you pass the kitchen where cooks are preparing supper. You realise that by tomorrow some people from your enterprise will have to cook the food.

It is like the secret workshop in Recife, Brazil, in the 1960s all over again. People have to ORGANIZE themselves to live together for a month.

The Crew Talks Business Only With the PE

The crew members (the facilitators' enterprise, the 'coaches') will not tell participants what to do.

They will not talk business with individual participants.

They will not talk business with individual work teams.

The crew will talk business only *with the organization/enterprise of the participants, or its representatives*. They will negotiate with this organization. They will sign work contracts with the organization of the participants represented by its elected leaders.

Fortunately, the participants *do have* an organization. The Participants Enterprise was formed late last night after the second day of the OW.

Let´s backtrack to the second day.

It was agreed early on the second day that nobody would quit until the PE was formed. By 4 on the second afternoon, people realized that there was a long way to go. Each proposal about the way to organize was supported by some but questioned by others. Everything was up for debate. What do we call our enterprise? Should we allow smoke breaks? Will there be one catering team or do we take turns cooking? How many signatories should there be on the bank account? Can the committee spend money earned by the enterprise without consulting the general meeting? How do we manage the storeroom?

The meeting went on until past midnight. By 1 a.m. the newly elected chair of the enterprise suggested that everyone should get some sleep while he, the deputy chair and the secretary put together all the agreements into a constitution. At 7a.m. on the third morning the participants gathered to find the weary chair and secretary waiting with the constitution.

They had done a good job in putting the agreements into a good sequence. Each clause was read out and approved by a show of hands. Afterwards all participants signed the resolution adopting the constitution. By this time it was mid-morning and the tired chair led the elected committee members to go and fetch the OW director and crew. One way or another the participants had *Organized* themselves. They did it themselves; the crew did not tell them what to do.

While waiting for the committee to come back with the directors the participants started to celebrate, dancing and singing. A song came up, which mentioned the name of the new enterprise. Even those who had argued for another name sang happily. Spirits were high.

When the crew arrives with the committee, the director thanks everyone for the constitution and the resolution that shows it has been approved by all members of the enterprise. Then he says there is one question that the crew would like answered before recognizing the enterprise, because the constitution does not answer it at all: How is the committee accountable to the members of the enterprise, and what can members do if they are unhappy with the committee's actions? *The crew leaves the meeting and for another 2 hours participants discuss until they find agreements about this matter, and put in a new page that sets out these points. After this the crew is called again. The director shakes hands with the chair while everyone cheers, claps and whistles. Then the handover of tools and vehicles, money and offices begins. ...*

The participants feel good about the enterprise they have formed. Later they may experience difficulties that will lead them to change their minds and re-organize their organization. In most Organization Workshops they do.

Later the participants may remove the leaders they have elected and replace them with other leaders. In most Organization Workshops they do.

Some Problems Maybe Nobody Thought of

Looking over the offers of work contracts posted on the walls, some of the participants tell the committee that they want to form a construction team to take on a contract to build an extension on the bakery. They point out the job and give their names to the chair, and he takes down the work description from the wall so that the committee can take it into negotiations with the crew. He takes responsibility for negotiating a contract but doesn't realise that he has no real idea of the job.

The skilled builders who read the offer on the wall wait outside to hear about the contract. Inside the director asks the committee whether it would like to call the builders to advise it on costs and process. "No" says the committee; "we are the ones who will enter the contracts!" The director shrugs and goes ahead. Later when the builders see the contract and realise the price is low they storm into the crew office. "You are cheating us!" they shout. The director puts up a hand requesting to speak. "Your committee signed that contract. We will not talk to you individually, only through your representatives. Kindly talk to the committee and if you want changes, let them come and negotiate them!"

The crew only does business with the PE (Participants Enterprise).

Maybe somebody thought of this problem last night when the participants were organizing themselves. Maybe they thought of establishing a procedure for getting the skilled workers to advise the committee, or to be present at the contract negotiation.

But maybe nobody thought of it. Maybe this is a detail of organization that still needed to be worked out. As a result of this incident it does get worked out.

Participants learn organization by achieving organization, not through following instructions.

Something else maybe nobody thought of is this: Maybe there are more skilled builders in the team, not only the four who spoke to the committee. Maybe the enterprise can take on three building jobs. *But nobody knows about them.* The participants *enterprise* may not know about the skills of its own members.

Another problem: *There is only enough food in the pantry for three days.* Everyone knows about taking over the cooking on the fourth day, but nobody has planned the meals.

The participants may find some way to get food. They have working capital and so can send the driver to buy food. But there will be no breakfast and lunch may be late on the fourth day. When working capital finishes and the first contracts have not been finished the problem of hunger comes up again. What does the enterprise do now to get food? Nobody had thought this far… *A quiet woman who has been elected secretary makes a proposal: Why not ask the crew for an emergency loan to buy food, to be repaid immediately the first contracts are paid? The committee sits down to prepare for this negotiation with the crew.*

Another problem maybe nobody thought of: *When the jobs are done and invoiced and the cash is put in the PE account, what is to be done with it?* How much money will be paid over to the people who actually did the work on the job? How does the Committee earn money? How do the cooks in the kitchen get paid? How much money must be put aside to buy food, and to repay the emergency loan for food?

The PE may want to request instruction or technical backup in accounting to help it plan for good financial management. But at the beginning it may not think about doing this.

Maybe nobody thought about problems like this in the middle of the night when the *enterprise* was first *organized*. Then again, maybe somebody did but was not taken seriously. Either way, as the problems come up and have to be dealt with, the participants will find a way to *organize themselves* to deal with them. They always do.

The First Lectures

By the third day we have already been through two lectures coming from Clodomir de Morais´ *Notes toward a Theory of Organization*.

The first was about the origins of the organization of labour. It is done with slides and references to local realities by the director who gives the lecture and by the participants who discuss it. *The participants are encouraged to comment, ask questions and talk.*

Excerpts from the First Lectures

The Cradle of Humankind was in Africa.

From here human beings expanded over thousands of years to the rest of the world.

Throughout history humans have organized to sustain themselves.

At the beginning of history humans survived by hunting, fishing, and gathering. Human communities were nomadic, following the animals or seeking plants to gather. We did not have a fixed place of residence. Caves sometimes gave shelter from storms and protection from wild animals.

Labour was divided according to people's biological characteristics. There were different tasks for women and for men, for the elderly and for children.

Men were responsible for hunting, and for defence of the group.

Women stayed near the camp since they looked after the children. They performed many jobs apart from child care: Food preparation and processing, gathering medicine from plants and caring for sick or hurt people, making utensils, working animal skins and furs to make clothing. *(This point always sparks a discussion.)*

All evidence shows that there was spirituality from the very early times.

(Sometimes participants share their knowledge about surviving remnants of older forms of organization, either from their own experience or learned from elders in their childhood, or passed down in the form of stories.)

The role of a woman allowed her to discover agriculture and husbandry. She noticed that discarded seeds sometimes grew, and learnt how to plant and reap. She noticed that animals came near to get the scraps of food thrown away by humans, and learnt to domesticate them. In addition to all her other work, woman thus carried knowledge of agriculture. The economy depended on the knowledge and skills of women. Women fed the tribe during periods of shortage. The many roles played by women meant that they became leaders in society; our thinking patterns, our minds, are shaped by our activities. *(This point always sparks discussion.)*

All evidence suggests that all ancient societies were led by women. Men's leadership came much later, as we shall see. *(More discussion …)*

There was a gradual transition from a hunter-gatherer way of life to agriculture. People started to settle in one place. Numbers of people grew. There was now a social division of labour, with some groups farming and others herding animals.

With more time, and with a surplus of food some people paid more attention to crafts like weaving, pottery, tool-making – and specialisation developed steadily over the years. Society became hierarchical. For the first time there were armies, where young men were put to service to perform tasks, or to fight on behalf of the tribe.

Practical Learning Exercise

At one time in his life Howard was a lawyer for the famous Mexican-American labour organizer Cesar Chavez. Cesar used to say, *"If you want to organize people, you have to give them something to do. If they don't have something to do, they will lose interest and drop out".*

Think about the people in the organizations you are in, or about the community you are trying to organize. Does everybody have something to do?

Are there useful tasks that are not being done by anyone?

Chapter Six: Unbounded Organization

In the OW lectures the participants learn to see the organization of their own work as part of the long history of the organization of labour on the planet earth. As they reflect on what was done at different times of humankind's history they see that some of the ways we organize now – for work, as part of religion, or just to celebrate social occasions – have been around for thousands of years.

Participants also begin to see the new patterns of organization that have developed over the last few centuries and even *the last few decades*. Of course this is unusual because most people do not even consider that there are different ways to think about organization.

> Starting in the last half of the 20th century, one particular way of thinking about organisation has been dominant. We can call this "bounded organisation".
>
> All those inside an organization work for a specific goal, and follow its rules and values. We talk about the organisation's members or staff, and about everyone else as being 'outside' the organisation. We talk about an organisation's "core competence", its "competitive advantage" and its "unique selling proposition".
>
> The organisation focuses on its core purpose and may not notice anything else; it sees itself as the centre of the universe rather than part of a family of organizations. Anything to do

> with society or the environment is seen as an externality; at best it is seen as the responsibility of government.
>
> Business operates like this.
>
> Non-profit organisations operate like this.
>
> Even government departments may operate like this.
>
> The imagination is that if all organisations do well, then society will do well. Sadly this is not true. But this way of thinking sees destruction of the environment as no company's business. Inequality is not any organization's business. ...

The OW participants start to understand a general principle: Every enterprise exists on two "enterprise planes".

On the first plane every enterprise has its own goals, and it works to achieve them. On the second plane it aligns with the goals of the SOCIETAL ENTERPRISE. It contributes to social goals like ending poverty, caring for the environment, fighting racism and respecting human rights.

This insight by participants has practical consequences.

Once we start to identify with the societal enterprise, we also recognise that most people have grown used to seeing only their immediate bounded enterprises. We learn to think and act with others in society for mutual benefit: this may result in cooperation with individuals in other organizations or those who do not even belong to an organization; this may bring a partnership with another company, or club, or a part of government. Increasingly people start to look at the big picture no matter what we do. We do not accept the easy assumption that major issues facing society will only be addressed by government. Over time we learn how to involve others in action to address 'big picture' issues; we learn new kinds of activity. And this new activity at a local level can also inspire conversation and organization at other levels of society.

The recognition that we like others have been 'trapped' in one model of organization also opens eyes in other ways. We start to realise that there are other "learned disabilities", where habits and teaching have narrowed or blocked our vision; we notice that some of the 'truths' we have been given about other things may not be the only truth. It becomes easier to think "outside the box"; outside the frameworks that have been given us as common sense and absolute truth.

We are liberated from being prisoners of conventional thinking or "common wisdom"; we are free to consider all options.

In the weeks of the OW the participants do not just learn about thinking outside the box in lectures and discussions. They *live* it.

They live the freedom to organize their work as they see fit; to construct together what works best for them; to learn from experience, and on the basis of this experience re-organize in whatever way may be needed to get the job done. This is all done within their bounded enterprise, but as they forge agreements and partnerships to cope with the many tasks to be done – and as they interact with others in their community to discuss what might be done differently in the future – they start to catalyse learning across the wider society. Their energy finds focus in new organizing options and new visions of possibility. We will describe later how participants in the Bokfontein OW decided to re-organize the layout of their settlement, to create public spaces where before there had been only private spaces. We will see that they came to share a Pan-African perspective where people with different ethnic and national identities live together in harmony.

These participants realised the truth of what we said very early in this book: what we do in our little corners of the world can make a difference for the whole world. We can all participate in defining and learning our way into the future.

By being part of an enterprise that inspires purposeful activity and collaborative initiatives with others in our social environment, we start to live Unbounded Organization.

The concept of Unbounded Organization can be thought of as an invitation to create a system of activities that give expression to the full potential of humanity. Whatever the ideas in our heads may be, our practical activities on the ground are interlinked and interdependent with the activities of many others. The concept of Unbounded Organization invites us to open what is in our heads to the interdependent world in which our practice is happening.

It is based on a few general principles.

The first general principle is "dream BIG but deliver on everything (small) you set out to do".

- Dream of reversing global warming but deliver on planting trees.

- Look to change the world but have a detailed work plan for the next months.
- Attack poverty but make sure your bounded enterprise succeeds financially.

A second principle is to mobilize all possible allies for a programme or change process.

- Start with those most affected by an issue, or those who are currently tackling it; ask how good initiatives can be expanded.
- Work for 'big picture' clarity: discuss what can be achieved and the specific actions that would contribute to this. Ask for suggestions, and build on them.
- Don't hold on to a good idea, allow others to participate; form partnerships.
- Formal coalitions may be possible sometimes, but informal collaboration across organizational boundaries and social 'sectors' is also vital for change to happen.

In every OW there is an effort to bring a wide range of actors into collaborative activity: business, local government, political activists, church leaders, women and youth groups and many others. This merely takes further and organizes around a natural impulse of any social initiative to 'involve others'.

A third principle is to catalyse societal learning. Crucially we are challenged to learn new kinds of activity. If we see that unemployment is a feature of society, we can't just hope that jobs will appear. We have to create new patterns of work and learn new ways of organizing that give meaning to life.

In short we must learn activities that allow expression of humanity's genius. Of course learning is necessary also within *organizations.* An organization that cannot learn cannot correct its mistakes. To survive it must learn at least as fast as its environment changes. *At the individual level we can say that lifelong learning is the calling of every human being.*

Finally there is the principle: Think Outside the Box! (And act in innovative "outside the box" ways!)

Thinking outside the box is an advanced way to be reasonable. It is reasonable to consider a wide array of options before deciding what to do; non-conventional options as well as the normal and conventional ones. It is reasonable to be open to learning from experience.

It is unreasonable to process experience by trying to fit everything you are learning inside the "box" of the ideas you already have.

For example: A young man named Cesar Chavez got a grant to organize a union of farm workers in California. When his grant ran out his union collapsed. Then he got another grant and the same thing happened. In this case "the box" was the common idea that you cannot do anything until you get funding to do it. Then he got another idea "outside the box." He had the farm workers themselves pay him dues so he could organize them. Although each farm worker paid only a very small amount each week, the total was enough that he could live on it if he slept in a sleeping bag on his sister´s front porch. Today Cesar Chavez is so famous that his picture is on a USA postage stamp.

Think of it this way: As long as we keep doing the same old things the same old ways we can expect the same old results.

Do you see our point? More and more people do. *Every day more people realize that there are no solutions to society's intractable problems inside the box.* Every day there rise up more truly innovative solutions to concrete problems – *like water supply, child care, drug abuse, employment, health issues, crime* – in many places around the globe. We need to learn from these innovative practices, *especially when* they challenge previous ways of organizing.

Unbounded Organization offers a general concept that brings awareness of our challenges and opportunities as humankind, and reminds us of our interdependence. It provides a framework for seeing how aligned activity to address specific problems *must and will* add up to transforming the system.

It is more than a concept. *It is a concept grounded in practical experience.*

First Practical Exercise: Questioning the Box

Interview five people you know. Ask them *why* in their opinion society is not yet working for the benefit of all, and in harmony with nature. Do not accept complaints for answers. Do not accept blaming someone for an answer. Try to get their opinion on *why* this is not happening. Then write notes for yourself to see what you have learnt.

Second Practical Exercise: A Practical Step Forward, Organizing a Personal Network

Here are four simple steps to build a core personal network. A core personal network is a group of people you can count on. You can count on them and they can count on you. Having a network makes you a stronger contributor to any organization or any community because wherever you go you take your connectedness with you.

1. Estimate how many people you can handle. A normal person cannot keep up with more than a hundred. A more realistic list might name fifty or even twenty.

Do not forget to include family when you estimate how many personal commitments you can handle without becoming overextended and disappointing people.

Family members take time and energy the same as anybody else. Usually they take more.

Of course you can relate to a much larger number of people on Facebook , Twitter and other kinds of e-mail. (but of course you may not speak personally to many of them.) Howard regularly sends messages to over three thousand.

2. For each person on your list write down contact details and the names of key persons in their life. Write down what you know of their interests, and any ideas you have about how you can support them in this. Put their birthdays on your calendar. Remember them on their birthdays.

Make a file for this purpose. Keep it up to date. *Do not be overconfident about how much you can remember automatically just in your head without deliberately writing things down.*

3. Review your list every two months. *Is a relationship dying because you have not done anything together or communicated?* Do something. Communicate.

4. When somebody rejects you look on the bright side. If you want to be close to them, that does not necessarily mean they want to be close to you. If you can handle thirty and ten dump you, then you have twenty living commitments *and ten free slots for making new friends.* If you can handle ten and you lose five, then you have five free slots.

These four steps do not deal with the deeper issues. They do not deal with the deeper issues of how to find loyal friends and soul-mates. They do not deal with how to align the actors in an activity system in creative outside-the-box ways.

But by taking care of some housekeeping details these four steps free you up to deal with the deeper issues.

Third Practical Learning Exercise

Talk with three colleagues, and ask yourselves the question: What pattern of activities can we create together (or at least start) that will be nurturing of society, or the environment?

Chapter Seven: Unbounded Community Development

Two main experiences led Gavin to the idea of unbounded organization. One was his experience in organization workshops. The other was his experience as a staff member and manager of non-profits, like the one in Botswana mentioned earlier. He noticed that each organization only paid attention to its own core purpose, and seldom noticed what else was happening in the places in which it worked.

Once you have the idea of unbounded organization you can apply it to community development. You can take an unbounded approach to community development.

An unbounded approach seeks to align all actors to serve the common good. It seeks to bring into one organizing path those who are in youth clubs and women's groups, those without any organization at all, those who work for government or private companies and of course those who are unemployed.

An unbounded dimension of a community is time. Communities grow out of their past and into an indefinite future that has no ending point. Sometimes they need to get back in touch with their past to learn who they are and what their ancestors stood for and believed. This kind of alignment is a source of deep strength.

What is possible in a community is only what the community is ready for. Development needs roots in what people understand.

It needs roots in what people want. It needs roots in who people trust.

For example: one community may be ready to call a meeting and brainstorm around what to do about crime. A second community may not be there yet. In the second community there may be too much apathy and fear, too little confidence. If you called a meeting nobody would come.

Avoid calling meetings if you think the meeting will be a failure because very few people or nobody would come. Nothing fails like failure. If you do call a meeting and you are unsure of attendance, consider holding it in a small room. The crowd will seem bigger if the space is smaller.

In fact a meeting can be two or three people working out what to do next. Then over time a working group forms that eventually raises the interest of many people to act on an issue, or to start imagining a better future.

A community has to grow from within. If there is no buy-in, no ownership, nothing will happen. If there are no inside change agents there will be no change.

If you do not live in the community, be careful about treating the first people who volunteer to work with you as potential change agents. They may be natural leaders respected by all, but on the other hand they may be outcasts who have no friends so they latch onto you.

If you have lived in your community all your life, you already know something about who the leaders are. You already know something about which messengers can deliver which messages. You already know that if X says something few will listen, but if Y says the same thing it will be taken seriously. But don't assume that you are always correct!

Every community is different. For example, in the 1970s Howard had a method that worked well in Chile. When he was called to Central America, to Honduras, he found that the method that worked in Chile did not work in Honduras. He had to re-learn.

A theory used in organization workshops that applies to community development is activity theory. Activity theory tells us that to work in a community you should be in touch with the whole activity system, in other words, with all the people and things that interact with each other in that place –employers and workers, unemployed, police, churches, the councilors, healers, those who gather at places of entertainment, tuck shops, spaza shops, supermarkets, petrol stations, hawkers who sell on the street, addicts, political parties, hospitals, taxi drivers, self employed handymen, coaches and players, schools, children, youth, women, men, adults, senior citizens and so on – the whole shebang.

Activity theory also tells us that attitudes change through activity. So by all means do something. Remodel a building. Plant a community garden. Start a crime watch. Join a choir and learn to sing. Learn a new dance. Clean house for someone sick with AIDS. Get together a sewing circle to alter hand-me-down clothes that no longer fit kids who outgrew them. Bake for a bake sale. Fix bicycles. Clean up the park. Glean the food that farmers leave in the fields because it does not pay them to harvest it and preserve the food for winter. Lift weights. Run a marathon.

Nothing dissolves apathy like activity. Apathy melts in activity like ice cubes melt in the sun.

Four Practical Exercises

First Exercise: Study What Is in the People's Heads

Of course you can never get all the way into the heads of all the people in the community and see what ideas are in them. But there are two things you can do:

1. Take notes on what *comes out of* people's heads when they talk. Write down *their exact words.* You cannot write down everything they say so you have to select. Select words that you keep hearing again and again as you study the community. Select what seems to be important to people.

4. Take notes on *what goes into* people's heads when they watch television. Do not watch just any TV programme. Watch what everyone else is watching. Do the same with whatever else is putting ideas into people's heads: video games, sermons, words in traditional ceremonies, political speeches, popular songs everybody listens to … whatever is forming minds by putting ideas in minds.

Then when you speak to people use what you learned listening and taking notes. You will be glad you noted *their exact words* instead of paraphrasing in your own words. Because then you can be sure they understand you. You return to them what they gave to you.

Second Exercise: Take Notes on Energies. In Other Words, Take Notes on Emotions and Feelings

This is harder than copying down words. You have to detect the energy and then write down something that will remind you of what you detected when you read your notes.

Use your own body as a scientific instrument. Listen with the heart. Tune in with your whole body. Resonate to how people feel.

Notice other people's body language, especially the eyes. Notice when people's eyes glisten, or open wide, or get teary.

Pay attention to commercials on television. When a big company spends big money for ads it is because they have good information about what energies will move people to pay attention to the ad and to buy their product. You will probably encounter the Big Six: sex, love, fear, nostalgia, pride, laughs. Do not underestimate nostalgia.

If you want to start a community project but there is no energy moving it but your own, forget it. Nothing moves without energy. Do not be stubborn about giving up your favourite idea for an initiative if it lights no fires.

When you find a vein of energy that really excites people, think about how to channel that energy into ways to build community bonds or linkages and move the community forward. When you organize an event make it fun. Make it moving.

Third Practical Exercise: Brainstorm Possible Projects by Connecting Gifts

For this exercise you will need small cards to write on, pencils or pens to write with, sellotape, and a meeting room where nobody will complain if you tape cards to walls.

Pass out cards. Then talk about different kinds of gifts people have. Ask people to write names for their gifts on cards -- one gift per card.

Start with Gifts of the Heart. A gift of the heart is a natural inclination to enjoy doing something. Some people have a gift of the heart for working with young children. Others have a gift for caring for sick people who are bedridden. Some have a passion for gardening, or for mechanics, or reggae, or rugby.

Gifts of the Hands are things you can do with your hands, like carpentry, or cooking, or TV repair, or plumbing, or making dresses.

Gifts of Experience is a place to fit in jobs people have worked at, or any experience that has given them skills, wisdom, or knowledge.

Gifts of People in my Life would include useful contacts.

Gifts of Things would include houses, vehicles, and tools.

Play with the idea of gifts, thinking of different kinds of gifts people might have in the place where you are. At one place there might be Gifts of Cattle. At another Gifts of Musical Talent.

Do not forget gifts that belong to institutions, like a building in the neighborhood that belongs to a church, or a vacant lot that belongs to a hospital, or government programmes. These can be resources available to the community for projects. You might write these cards yourself.

People may express gratitude for their gifts. Sometimes the whole meeting can turn into testimonies about God's blessings, or praise of mothers, or gratefulness for having children who are so good to their parents. Go with the flow.

You can help people who have difficulty writing, if it does not embarrass them. Or a daughter or friend can help.

Then when the gifts are written on cards TAPE THE CARDS TO THE WALLS.

Then people walk around the room reading the cards, taking them down, taping them up again in new combinations. Put cards next to each other when putting them together suggests possibilities for cooperation.

Moving the cards on the walls around helps to connect gifts.

For example, if there are rooms in a church that are vacant most of the week, and people with Gifts of the Heart or Gifts of Experience working with small children, and a van, then you have the makings of a crèche.

You may have the makings of a dance troupe, or a farmers fresh produce market, or a barbershop or beauty salon, or an AIDS hospice, or a youth rugby club. There is no limit, which brings us back to our magic word UNBOUNDED.

Fourth Practical Exercise: A Homework Assignment

Look up "activity theory" on the Internet.

Chapter Eight: Alignment

When you align with someone you and the other person work towards the same goals. When an organization aligns with another organization the two organizations work for the same goals.

In the first part of this book we shared about organization workshops. That led to the idea of unbounded organization. Once you have the unbounded organization idea you can apply it to community development at a local level. The people in the neighbourhood align to work for the same goals, even if they are working on slightly different things. We wrote about that in the previous chapter.

You can also take an unbounded approach at the level of ALL OF SOCIETY. Then everybody in society aligns to pursue the same goals like, for example, reduce, re-use, recycle.

Another example would be the constitution of a country. The constitution defines values the whole country is supposed to align with. International treaties align the entire world to commit to human rights.

We can think of society as the SOCIETAL ENTERPRISE. The idea is that all of society is one big complex enterprise. We are all in it together. Unfortunately the way we normally organize we do not recognize this, so we may not see that we have similar goals and values.

In an unbounded approach you do not make your own personal plans as if you were the centre of the universe and everybody else and everything else revolved around you. A company or a non-profit or a public ministry does not act as if it were the centre of the universe either.

When you think in an unbounded way you do not exaggerate your own importance, although of course you still remain true to your values and passion.

You align at every level. You align with your family and friends. You align with your neighbourhood. You align with your country. You align with the human rights of all human beings. You align with our mother the earth.

Here is a related point: What we do to change our little corner of the world makes change in the whole world. The change may be small, but it is real. Small changes add up. The world is an interconnected system. Since the world is an interconnected system, when we make changes in our neighborhood, the changes have a ripple effect in all the other neighbourhoods all around the world. In an interconnected system whatever happens in a part makes a difference for the whole.

In the OW lectures participants learn that every enterprise exists on two "enterprise planes". On the first plane every enterprise has its own goals. On the second plane it aligns with the goals of the SOCIETAL ENTERPRISE. It serves social goals like ending poverty, harmony with the environment, and respect for human rights.

What does it take to align? It takes a shared vision. A common dream. People are empowered to cooperate effectively toward reaching common goals because they share a vision. They share understandings. Because of the common dream they share energies. On a neighbourhood level we can share a vision for our neighbourhood.

On a national level Nelson Mandela had a vision for South Africa: "a non-racial society with respect for all and justice for all". Millions shared the vision and aligned with it across all sectors of society, all races, all religions, all ages.

You could call Mandela's vision a historical vision. It was a shared vision because millions aligned to it. It played a role in history.

If we look back at the past, we see other shared historical visions. For example, nearly a thousand years ago building a great cathedral in a European country like France or Spain was a huge collective effort. The time from start to finish could be as long as five generations. Cathedrals people admire today were built long ago by people with a shared historical dream and vision "to build something beautiful for God".

It is not possible to have a shared vision unless there is a shared story: an understanding about where we came from and what kinds of futures we may create. A shared story that runs through time, a 'metanarrative', can powerfully influence everyday behaviour. This is why it is so important to challenge myths that may get spread by laziness in the media or through the deliberate peddling of falsehoods. A feature of the 21st century is that for almost every 'story' representing a set of facts, there is a contesting story, suggesting the opposite. As an example, a well-known comedian in the USA noted that although 97% of all scientific articles about climate change showed that this is a man-made phenomenon, the media always treats the evidence as if "one person says this, and one person says that" so that as a society we never realise that in fact there is overwhelming evidence about our use of fossil fuels harming the environment.

So the creation of a common story is not as simple a matter as it might have been in previous centuries. It involves a decision to think independently. Remember what we asked from you at the beginning of this book? We asked for *Realism*, to see the world as it is: Even when reality is different from what the mainstream media and the dominant culture say it is, and even when reality is different from what we ourselves wish were true.

With a shared vision people are capable of great achievements. Without a shared vision there is less communication. There is less alignment. There is less coming together to do things that we cannot do alone.

Here is a smaller example of alignment with a shared vision:.

Howard once worked with community organizers among rural people scattered across a rainy landscape in the south of Chile. The shared vision was "building a better future for our children".

School teachers, mothers, fathers, priests and pastors, media, doctors and nurses, farmers, workers, shopkeepers, business people, hawkers, and unemployed alcoholics aligned with the vision.

Organizing *For* Rather Than Organizing *Against*

Aligning with a shared historical vision is organizing *for* something to happen. It is not just organizing *against*. Much of the spontaneous organization that occurs in communities or across society in social movements is organization *against* injustice or abuse of power. The trouble is that very often it is not so easy to move from organizing against something to create a better future.

For example, some people align with a vision of "zero poverty" going from door to door looking for problems to solve like widows without food and children without parents. They mobilize resources to meet needs. They do something to solve the problem. They praise more than they complain.

There are urban neighbourhoods in Argentina where people judge the sincerity of believers of different religions and members of different political parties by how they do or do not cooperate with those most in need. If you do not show solidarity with the poor nobody believes you when you talk about your religious or political creed.

There are many other ways to align with "zero poverty". Scientists do research. Politicians build alliances and design policies. Business people (we mean socially responsible business people) strive to deliver quality products at affordable prices. Mothers and fathers help their children with their homework so that their children will escape poverty themselves and will be able to serve society. Whoever we are, whenever we work against poverty we are aligning with the societal enterprise. Citizen organizations show governments and big corporations in very detailed ways what they need to do to change structural problems – and mobilize for this to happen.

Most societies today envision "zero poverty" and "living green" as goals. Many different people align to work for such goals. Each of us has the opportunity to paint a small part of the big picture of a better future for all.

A shared historical vision makes us a "we". It makes us no longer just a collection of separate isolated individuals who happen to be in the same place at the same time.

Practical Exercises

The first two practical exercises are about alignment to a shared vision that at this point in history humanity must unite to save our mother earth and specifically to reverse global warming.

First Practical Exercise: Planting Trees

Planting trees is a good activity for creating positive energy and giving people a personally rewarding sense of alignment with the common good. It is a way to align with "save the planet from global warming". Trees take carbon dioxide out of the air and put oxygen into the air. When the air has more oxygen and less carbon dioxide the sun´s rays arriving at the earth's atmosphere produce less heat. When the air has more carbon dioxide and less oxygen the sun's rays arriving at the earth's atmosphere produce more heat. Currently the air on planet earth has more than 400 parts per million. According to the trend already in motion it does not seem possible to stop its rise short of 550. But 550 is too much. 400 is already too much. The earth is getting warmer. The water supply is dwindling, leading to loss of farmland to desertification.

Planting trees makes up for the forests that have been cut down. It puts oxygen back into the air. It takes carbon dioxide out of the air.

(However, global warming is just one source for global warming and too much carbon dioxide is bad for life for more reasons than its contribution to global warming.)

Second Practical Exercise: Keep Bees, or Run an Organic Garden

For those who can, another way to align with "save the planet from global warming" is to keep bees.

Bee populations are falling as pollution is rising, as well as the use of chemical pesticides. Much of plant life and much of the human food supply depends on bees, because bees pollinate plants, enabling them to produce food.

If bees go extinct, we go too.

Whether or not it is practical for you to keep bees, you may be able to tend an organic (or "natural") garden. You may be able to start one or join a group (or family) that runs one.

In many cities people do natural gardening on rooftops or on vacant lots.

Natural gardening restores the worms, the microorganisms, and the organic matter to the soil.

Third Practical Exercise: A Topic for Discussion

We wrote:

"What we do to change our little corner of the world makes change in the whole world. The change may be small, but it is real. Small changes add up. The world is an interconnected system. Since the world is an interconnected system, when we make changes in our neighborhood, the changes have a ripple effect in all the other neighbourhoods all around the world. In an interconnected system whatever happens in a part makes a difference for the whole".

Do you believe this?

Fourth Practical Exercise: Two Questions

If it is so clear that alignment is needed, why is there so little of it?

Why is there not more alignment?

Chapter Nine: Meetings

Every organization has meetings. Success depends on the quality of the meetings.

Meetings for Business

A business meeting makes decisions.

An individual or a small committee *prepares the meeting* by preparing the *documents for the meeting*.

The documents might include:

1. The agenda.
2. A financial report on money coming in and money going out.
3. A critical balance reporting on a recent event, workshop, or other activity. The critical balance should answer the questions: What went well? Why? What went wrong? Why? Based on this what do we need to do to improve our organization?
4. Proposals or work plans for coming activities.
5. Letters and memos received, for example a letter from the mayor.
6. Minutes of the last meeting.

7. Background information on decisions to be taken. As an example, three quotes on the cost of paint needed to paint a school.
8. Other useful background information.

THE DOCUMENTS SHOULD BE CIRCULATED IN ADVANCE OF THE MEETING. A meeting can only be as good as the preparation for it.

Beginning the Meeting

We recommend beginning a meeting with an ice-breaker. This can be any combination of the points below. What is chosen will depend on what is practical, considering the number of people in the meeting:

1. Refreshments with handshakes, hugs and small talk.
2. A prayer or benediction.
3. A song.
4. A short welcoming speech reminding people of the values and purposes of the organization, and of where this particular meeting fits into the big picture.
5. "New and good". This consists of each member sharing something that is new and good in her or his life.

Make sure everyone who arrives is properly greeted and made to feel welcome. Pretend everyone has a sign on their forehead that says, "Make me feel important".

When people sit down for business give them some time to review the documents. Then spend a few minutes reviewing the agenda. The agenda is supposed to express the collective will of the group even though for reasons of convenience it was drawn up by one person or by a small committee. Amend the agenda if necessary to get agreement on it.

Running the Meeting

Now you are ready to take up each item on the agenda.

There may be some formal agenda items that can be quickly agreed on. Do not get into a discussion where none is necessary.

Should there be a time limit for speaking? For example each person who wants to speak could get up to two minutes to discuss the first agenda item.

Whether there should be time limits depends on how the people in the group feel. Some people love it when the chair runs a tight ship, allowing only so much time per item and asking for rapid agreement on decisions. Other people hate it. Time limits drive them crazy. Time limits make them angry.

For most groups a good chair will find a happy medium, politely suggesting approximate time limits. The chair will not enforce time limits strictly, but will nonetheless gently get people back on track when they wander off the subject or talk too long. When silences occur it may be important for the chair to 'listen' to them, to observe the body language in the room and then to reflect back to the meeting where the discussion has taken it.

While the chair is chairing, the secretary is busy taking notes on what is being said. She or he does not try to write down everything, but only to get the gist of the main points.

The chair should turn to the secretary when it appears that the time has come to end discussion on an item. Then the secretary should use her or his notes to summarize what has been said, doing the best she or he can to give a fair account of the ideas expressed. It is not necessary and usually not desirable to personalize the summary by saying who said what. It is the ideas that should be summarized.

Some members may want to add something or subtract something from the secretary's summary.

Ending the Meeting

Try to make decisions by consensus. Everyone should agree.

If all goes well the secretary's summary on an agenda item, plus any amendments people may wish to add, should lead to a logical conclusion. The decision will be made by logic, not by one faction imposing its will on another. When a vote is necessary it is often wise to put off a decision until the next meeting. In the interval between one meeting and the next learning more facts and reflecting more on ideas may produce a logical conclusion everyone can agree on.

When there is agreement, the action should be set out as part of a plan, where there is a record of the agreed action, who will do it, when it needs to be completed, and what resources the organization is allocating to the actions.

Everyone should accept responsibility for carrying out the decisions made at the meeting.

Particular individuals should commit to particular actions.

Before the meeting is over it should choose a person to be what the English call a "whip" and what the Argentines call a "counsellor of the meeting", or what may be called in Setswana "motshwaraganyi" – the one who pulls things together. This is a person in charge of following up the decisions by reminding the others. "You promised X by date Y. Where is it?"

The whip should have a strong personality. But even people who are not normally assertive can play the role of "check" or "control" because they know that they are simply enforcing the decision of the group. Where there is no control as a follow-up, things do not get done and organizations go downhill.

Meetings for Learning

Although meetings for learning do not make decisions they are very important.

An organization that does not learn is unable to correct its mistakes.

It does not keep up to date.

To survive, an organization must learn at least as fast as its environment changes.

The people who are members of the organization are happier when they are learning.

A life without learning is not a human life as God and Nature intended.

Meetings for learning can be with invited people from outside as guest speakers, or guest teachers, or guest entertainers. Or they can be with people from inside the community as presenters. Or they can be discussions of videos downloaded from YouTube.

The first thing necessary for a successful series of learning meetings is to get people to come. Experience shows that people are most likely to come when they get a *personal invitation*. Let people know they are missed. Make them feel wanted. Give them recognition – for example with a certificate.

People are most likely to come back if when they get there it is fun. Serve refreshments. Sing. Dance. Fill the learning meetings with music.

Howard once participated in a very successful series of learning meetings called "The University of Life". Every Sunday evening an invited speaker addressed the topic "what I have learned from life". The meetings began with supper, continued with the speaker, and ended with music.

Often it helps to meet in a small room. The same number of people attending can feel like a successful meeting in a small room and feel like a failed meeting in a large room.

Tense Meetings

Conflict happens all the time.

Here is some advice on how to resolve conflicts:

1. Get the burning issues on the agenda for a business meeting.
2. Consider calling special meetings to work out heated conflicts.

3. Assure people who are upset that their issues are on the agenda and they will be heard.

4. The secretary of the meeting where the disputed issues are discussed should make a special effort to take good notes, and to demonstrate to all parties that they have been fairly understood. This may take repeated effort, since it is very likely that not all parties will be satisfied by the first attempt.

5. Repeat back to people what you hear them saying until they are satisfied that you have understood their point of view.

6. Try to find *the right thing to do*. This may mean moving from a *binary orientation,* where one idea opposes another so that someone is bound to be a loser, to a *ternary orientation* where focus is on the issue to be dealt with.

7. Try to find solutions that give people *what they really need*. Often it is possible to find a solution where everybody wins because they get what they really need.

8. Often it is impossible to find a solution where everybody gets what they demand, but if everybody can be helped to hear what others are saying, there is often a possibility of compromise. You can get the process started of everybody hearing everyone else. You yourself can be someone who listens carefully with the heart and with the head.

9. When you are frustrated and you do not know what to do, seek advice. Seek advice from people with experience. Seek advice from just about anyone who is willing to listen to the problem and help you to think about how to resolve it.

Practical Learning Exercises

First Practical Exercise: A Day-Long Meeting to Map a Community's Assets

One way to do community mapping consists of six steps:

Step One: Ask people to talk about what they like about their community. Especially in poor communities people often find it hard to think about strengths and assets. Start the process by helping people to see what they already have to work with and build on.

When introducing the question you can acknowledge that the community has problems. We all know that. But for now let's focus on the positive.

People should be seated restaurant-style in groups of six around tables. Each group should choose a scribe to take notes and a reporter to report. We suggest 15 minutes in groups, followed by a long interactive session with all tables talking about what they discovered. The chair of the meeting should take an active part, drawing out participants' ideas. The chair should encourage everyone to take pride in their community, to appreciate its assets, and to envision its potential.

Coffee Break.

Steps Two and Three can be done simultaneously.

Two: What skills, abilities, and talents are available in the community? Please note the link between this step and the 'gifts' exercise that we mentioned earlier.

Three: What groups and organizations are present in the community and what are they doing?

Again, people can first discuss in groups and write up notes and then discuss all together. If these steps are done simultaneously, half the groups should answer question two and half the groups should answer question three.

Lunch.

Step Four: Ask each group to make a picture of the community that shows what it looks like and its assets.

We suggest 40 minutes to make the picture and up to an hour for each group to present its picture. Ask questions about what is left out. Where is the police station? The taxi rank?

Step Five: Ask people to take a walk around the community and come up with ideas of what can be done make it an even better place to live. (If there was enough time this step could take a full day!)

Coffee Break. Step Six: Brainstorm about ways to use the assets and resources of the community more effectively. Talk about how much money goes in and out of the community, in what form and why. (On this last point it helps to prepare by gathering some information in advance of the meeting.)

Materials needed: Cards for each table with each key question written down. Flipchart with blank paper. For each table: Flipchart paper for the pictures, several markers, tape, crayons, coloured paper, scissors, and glue.

Second Practical Exercise: A Topic for Discussion

"The people who are members of an organization are happier when they are learning. A life without learning is not a human life as God and Nature intended."

Do you believe this?

Chapter Ten: Bokfontein Amazes the Nations

The settlement at Bokfontein was born in trauma.

In 2005 people who had been living near Hartbeesport Dam were evicted to clear space for upscale housing. They agreed to relocate to a place called Bokfontein. They were dumped on bare land that did not even have a supply of water. They lost everything.

In 2006 people living at Melodi were also forcibly evicted. They were accused of illegally occupying land that was designated by the government for building low cost housing. They too were dumped at Bokfontein, in the same space where the people from Harbeesport were already living.

Those who had arrived first regarded the newcomers as intruders. Violence ensued. It was violence that expressed the deep psychological wounds of people who had been humiliated and denied their human rights. It was also violent competition for scarce resources needed to satisfy basic necessities of life, like the water that was trucked in by the municipality on an irregular and unreliable schedule.

Alignment in Action

Following a successful OW in Munsieville in 2007, government officers approached Gavin Andersson to ask if it would be possible to use the same method in working with the people in

Bokfontein. After a first meeting with residents of Bokfontein at the end of 2007 Gavin pulled together a crew, bringing in Langi Malamba, Owen Stuurman, Leon Mdiya, and Gwashi Manavhela. The five crew members began community consultations at Bokfontein in early 2008.

They started by going around talking and listening in ways similar to those suggested in the practical exercises in this book, for example the one at the end of Chapter Four. They listened to community leaders as is recommended in Chapter Seven. They met the community as a group every Tuesday for three months; in formal meetings as well as in informal interviews, stories, jokes and talks. They conducted 'scoping walks', saw what was available, and what resources were already being brought to bear (as well as how they could be applied more effectively).

They heard of the pathologies and the strengths, the dreams and the complaints. They floated ideas as well as questions, and got deep into dialogues where they eschewed exaggerating their own importance as if the universe revolved around them. They made it clear to all they met that they had no special skills in agriculture, or building or water provision, but only understood one thing: how organization works.

Taking a cue from activity theory, they talked with all those who were part of the activity system, including mining houses, municipality, political parties, local churches and charities. They talked to people who had lost loved ones. As activity theory tells us, nothing changes hearts and minds like activity. Accordingly, the team made plans for an Organization Workshop in Bokfontein – after presenting the idea to the community, discussing it in depth with key parties, and being properly invited. They did "scoping" as is described in Chapter Four. They organized a great deal of hands-on work. Everybody in the settlement at Bokfontein was invited to the OW and a hundred and eighty participated. Unlike a bounded small-group-psychology approach, an unbounded organization approach is ready to work with large groups.

On the unbounded approach of the OW, the people are free to organize their work as they see fit, and then to re-organize when they see fit to re-organize. They learn organization by doing it.

In the process of organizing themselves for practical tasks, participants bonded as a community. The crowning glory of the deliberations of the community in the OW at Bokfontein was a decision to sink a bore hole far below the surface to tap into an underground aquifer. A team of specialists came to drill it. The participants laid the piping. At last a reliable supply of water! In the process they empowered themselves to run it and to administer the provision of water for the people on a daily basis. The same water irrigated a one hectare community garden that was established through the OW. From that day until now the community has maintained and paid for their bore hole water supply.

In the OW they did hands-on work. They also analysed the main problems of the community and organized themselves to cope with them: Crime, alcohol abuse, and division.

"Division" calls for some explanation. The community was divided because of how it began. It was divided between the first arrivals who had been evicted from Hartbeesport, and the second arrivals who had been evicted from Melodi. To make matters worse it was further divided by prejudice against foreigners from Zimbabwe, Malawi, Mozambique, Lesotho, and other places who had left their home countries hoping for a better life in South Africa. Some had come with the others from Hartbeesport. Some had come with the others from Melodi. Some came later.

The OW was a turning point where the members of the community began to have public discussions about the prejudices that divided them. People were encouraged to do self-introspection to look at the life histories that in most cases had fostered deep-seated anger. They overcame stereotypes together and built positive identities around communication, collective responsibility, high self-esteem, and empowerment. They came to share a vision of "working together for peace and prosperity". Their new shared vision was catalyzed by lectures in the Organization Workshop described in chapter four. People had learned to frame their stories as parts of the larger and longer story of the human family. Specifically the participants in the workshop learned that it was just a little over a hundred years ago that Europe divided Africa and created its present boundaries. They agreed it was senseless to fight over identities created by boundaries so new and so arbitrary.

To celebrate their new identity and their newly-forged unity they decided to give their community a new name: *Tshaba di Maketse* which means "the nations are amazed".

At the closing ceremony of the OW participants sang songs from Malawi, Mozambique, Zimbabwe, and Lesotho, as well as from South Africa. As it happened, the previous night in the outskirts of Johannesburg and elsewhere, peace in South Africa had been shattered by the beginning of the first of what would prove to be a series of waves of xenophobic violence.

The Next Steps Are Unbounded

Many of the outcomes at Bokfontein could not have been predicted. When you do unbounded organization you respond to circumstances and ideas that might not have been present when the initial plans were made.

During the OW an old man died because it was impossible for an ambulance to get to his shack. The shacks were huddled so tightly together that vehicles could not enter. This prompted the settlers to sit down to work out what kind of community they wanted to create. Two decisions emerged: First, there had to be an access road that would allow ambulances and other vehicles to enter. Secondly, they realized that one thing every individual craved was space, but this was something they could not have on their individual plots. As a result of these two realizations they designed a new physical plan for the settlement.

Twenty four shacks were moved to land in another part of the settlement so that the participants could create a road. Eleven more shacks were moved to create "Phola Park", a large recreation area right next to the one hectare garden. In the middle of Phola Park stand an old farm house converted to a multi-purpose centre and near it a new thatched house built to serve as a functions venue. Residents can book the thatched house for birthday parties, weddings, family gatherings, and communal events.

The Community Development Forum forged through the OW took responsibility for safety and security.

Among other projects they put together a crèche at the multi-purpose centre so as to care better for children and to free up women to seek income-earning activities. The same building houses a drop-in centre. Children come by the drop-in centre after school to get a good meal and to find a quiet place to do homework.

Bokfontein became one of many sites throughout South Africa of the Community Work Programme (CWP), which uses public employment to catalyse community development.

Over the years Bokfontein has passed several acid tests as new waves of xenophobic violence have spread across poor communities in South Africa. In contrast with many similar places and in contrast with its own past, Bokfontein has remained peaceful and united. Truly it has amazed the nations.

Practical Learning Exercise: A Community Time Line

> Ask an assembly to which everyone is invited when their community was founded. Does anybody know? Can we think of anybody outside this group who may know?
>
> Then divide into groups, ideally of six people each and in any case of not more than twelve, ideally seated around tables.
>
> The assignment to each group is to draw a time line from the year the community began to the present year. What made the community grow? Who came first? Who came later? When were there floods? Fires?

Violence? Political events? Strikes or protests? Who were the leaders? When was the school built? The hospital or clinic? The churches? The highway, dam, railroad, stadium, or other significant infrastructure? Were there memorable soccer matches or other great sports events or heroes? And so on.

We suggest allowing each group forty minutes to draw their time line.

Then invite each group to send a representative to display and explain its time line. Other members of the group and of the whole assembly should feel free to comment.

This activity usually generates a lot of energy. People enjoy reminiscing about the past and their roles in it. Whoever chairs the meeting will have to use tact and good judgment to be sure everyone has a chance to speak and to have fun telling stories, and at the same time to keep the meeting from dragging on too long.

Materials you will need: Butcher paper, markers.

Appendix: Suggestions for Further Reading

Check out the website www.unboundedorganization.org. There you will find:

- a video about Gavin´s childhood
- published articles about unbounded organization
- information about Organization Workshops (OWs) including reports on the Otse, Botswana, workshop mentioned briefly in this book and on other workshops that have been done in Africa
- Gavin´s dialogue *Looking Back to the Future: Conversations on Unbounded Organisation*
- and much more.

Community organizing at Bokfontein in North West Province is often regarded as a successful example. You can begin to learn more about it and other experiences by checking out the websites of the think-tank Trade and Industrial Policy Strategies www.tips.org.za; the website of the International Labour Organization www.ilo.org; the website of Seriti Institute www.seriti.org.za; the website www.polity.org.za and the Wikipedia article "Organization Workshop". Search under "Bokfontein," "Organization Workshop", and "Community Work Programme".

Buy on the Internet or borrow from a library or request on Interlibrary Loan:

Gavin Andersson, with the assistance of Howard Richards (2015), *Unbounded Organization: Embracing the Societal*

Enterprise. Pretoria, University of South Africa Press. This longer book goes into greater detail on topics mentioned in the present brief introduction. It includes discussions of the shortcomings of standard Organizational Development (OD) practice that led Gavin to formulate the concept of unbounded organization.

Raff Carmen and Miguel Sobrado (editors) (2000), *A Future for the Excluded. Job Creation and Income Generation by the Poor: Clodomir Santos de Morais and the Organization Workshops.* London, Zed Books. This book is also available as an eBook that can be read on the Kindle. It gives a thorough account of the political context of the origins of OW in Brazil and of its spread to the rest of South America and to other continents. It has twenty chapters by various authors including Ivan and Isabelle Labra, Gavin Andersson, Clodomir Santos de Morais, and Clodomir´s life partner Jacinta Castelo Branco Correia. The first of its four sections is titled, "Those who don´t eat and those who don´t sleep".

Howard Richards and Joanna Swanger (2006), *Dilemmas of Social Democracies.* Oxford, Rowman and Littlefield. Also available as eBook for the Kindle. Chapter 10, "Power and Principle in South Africa," provides an account of Nelson Mandela´s dilemma of choosing between the ANC programme and getting investment. This book also shows how similar dilemmas plagued other countries.

Howard Richards (2014), "Unbounded Organization and the Unbounded University Curriculum," a chapter in Patricia Inman and Diana Robinson (editors), *University Engagement and Environmental Sustainability.* Manchester UK: Manchester University Press. This chapter in a book on university reform addresses three questions: Who are we? Where are we going? How will we get there?

Paulo Freire (1968), *Pedagogy of the Oppressed*. When this classic was first published in English in 1970 it was clandestinely distributed and avidly read among South African anti-apartheid activists. It is available online in PDF format.

John McKnight (2013), *A Basic Guide to ABCD Community Organizing*. This and much else can be downloaded free from www.abcdinstitute.org/publications/downloadable. ABCD stands for Asset Based Community Development. McKnight was Barack Obama´s supervisor when Obama was a community development organizer in Chicago. He wrote a recommendation to get Barack into law school.

Howard Richards and Joanna Swanger (2008), "Culture Change, a Practical Method with a Theoretical Basis," a chapter in Joe Rivera (ed.) *Handbook for Building Cultures of Peace*. (New York, Springer Publishers)

Jeremy Rifkin (2014) *The Zero Marginal Cost Society*. (New York, Palgrave Macmillan). An essay on major trends in global capitalism today. It is also available as an eBook to read on the Kindle.

John Gibbs (2013) *Moral Development and Reality*. (Oxford, Oxford University Press). An up-to-date textbook reporting on psychological research on human moral development.

Selected books published by Dignity Press

Howard Richards

The Nurturing of Time Future

ISBN 978-1-937570-01-9

*Howard Richards,
Joanna Swanger*

Gandhi and the Future of Economics

ISBN 978-1-937570-29-3

Available at www.dignitypress.org or at major online and offline bookshops.

Dignity Press
World Dignity University Press

Selected books published by Dignity Press

Evelin Lindner

A Dignity Economy -
Creating an Economy That
Serves Our Planet and
Preserves Human Dignity
ISBN 978-1-937570-03-3

Hilarie Roseman

Generating Forgiveness and
Constructing Peace through
Truthful Dialogue

ISBN 978-1-937570-48-4

For the complete program please check
www.dignitypress.org.

Dignity Press
World Dignity University Press

Printed in February 2023
by Rotomail Italia S.p.A., Vignate (MI) - Italy